THE WHY BOOK OF GOLF

200 Practical Tips and Fascinating Facts
About Golf Traditions, Rules and Etiquette!

by William C. Kroen

PRICE STERN SLOAN
Los Angeles

Published by Price Stern Sloan, Inc.
11150 Olympic Boulevard, Suite 650
Los Angeles, California 90064

Printed in U.S.A.

10 9 8 7 6 5 4 3 2 1

Library of Congress Cataloging-in-Publication Data
Kroen, William C.
    The why book of golf / by William Kroen
        p.   cm.
    ISBN 0-8431-2982-4
    1. Golf   I. Title.
GV965.K66   1992
796.352—dc20   91-30872
                                                        CIP

To the members of the Furnace Brook Golf Club.

William C. Kroen holds a Ph. D. in Education and brings his knowledge of teaching techniques to the golf course. The author of *A Hacker No More*, a step-by-step guide to the unique program he used to knock more than twenty strokes off his game, Kroen has a thorough knowledge of the game of golf and the golf swing to prove it. He is currently a golf professional associated with Dunlop sports.

I would like to thank Bruce Hoster of Dunlop Sports, Diane Becker of the USGA, Tom Tehan and Joe Pagliaro for their kind assistance with this book.

Contents

The Game

Mark Twain called it "a good walk spoiled." Some twenty million Americans are locked into a love-hate relationship with it. We spend over a billion dollars per year on equipment alone; we study videotapes and read texts as if learning brain surgery; we hunch toward the TV as the announcer whispers in the common language of all who play the game. How did this national obsession come about? What is the history of this distinctive game?

Golf's true origin is as hazy as ancient history. It was the Scots, however, who organized the game on a playing field, gave it rules and provided the vocabulary that we so often use today in our Sunday foursomes. Whether it was a shepherd hitting stones with his staff or sailors knocking stones along the path to the town with a club, the glorious game as it has evolved is rich in tradition and lore. The things we say and do on the golf course often have deep roots, and knowing the history can add to our overall enjoyment of the great game of golf.

The Game

Why is golf so named?

The word "golf" comes from the German word *kolbe*, which means club. The name has been used for many games played with clubs (the Dutch game *kolven*, for example). A debate about the origin of golf has been ongoing: Did it begin with the Flemish game of *chole*, the French *jeu de mail* or the Roman game of *Paganica* (the game of countrymen)? No one knows. The Scots, however, were the first to play the game of golf as it is played today. The first recorded reference to golf came in an Act of Scottish Parliament in 1457 that forbade golf and "futeball" because Scotland was at war with England, and the government didn't want young men neglecting military training.

The Game

Why are sand traps called "bunkers"?

"Bunker" comes from the Scottish *bonker*, meaning a chest or box where coal is kept, usually dug into the side of a hill. Often, cows would graze in the marshlands adjacent to the old links courses, standing alongside the dunes and creating a depression that reminded Scottish players of these chests, and eventually these areas became known as bunkers.

The Game

Why is the word "bogey" used to describe a score of one over par?

The term comes from an imaginary Colonel Bogey of the Great Yarmouth Club in England. It is believed that a Major Charles Wellman, while playing against ground score (par), referred to failing to get par as "getting caught by the bogey man," a phrase from a popular eighteenth-century tune. The members of the club began referring to an imaginary new member, Colonel Bogey, who would always shoot even par. As the game spread to the United States, "bogey" was narrowed to represent a score of one over par on a hole.

Why is the word "birdie" used for a score of one under par on a hole?

According to *Golf Magazine*'s *Encyclopedia of Golf*, "birdie" was coined in the United States. In 1903 a certain A.H. Smith of Atlantic City is said to have remarked after holing out, "That's a bird of a shot!" The words "eagle" and "double eagle" are outgrowths of the bird reference.

The Game

Why are the spectators at a golf tournament called a "gallery"?

In British theaters the large balcony containing the cheaper seats is called a gallery. Over the years the term has come to signify the public in general.

The Game

Why is the Masters considered one of the Grand Slam tournaments?

The Masters is the only privately run tournament of the big four considered to be the Grand Slam of golf. The U.S. Open, the PGA Championship and the British Open are all run and sanctioned by national golf institutions. The Masters has attained its prestigious place in golf history and lore with a great course, excellent ambience, exclusiveness, tradition and careful promotion. Bobby Jones started the Masters in 1934 as a starting tournament for the pro tour as the pros headed north after the winter season in Florida. Jones was interested in showcasing his Augusta National Course by having the greatest players available test their games each spring as the magnolias blossomed. By invitation only, the Masters provides an atmosphere free of commercialism and dedicated to the art of golf. Clifford Robert, who ran the tournament from the thirties right up to 1980, maintained an elite aura in every respect of the tournament, from television coverage to clubhouse decorum. The Masters grew in respect and esteem over the years to its current position as one of the most coveted titles in the game.

The Game

Why are some tournaments called "opens"?

"Open" means that the tournament is open to both amateurs and professionals.

HOLE	1	2	3	4	5	6	7	8	9	10	11
LEADERS PAR	4	5	3	5	4	4	4	4	3	4	4
BURNS	7	7	7	6	6	6	6	6	6	5	5
GRAHAM D	5	6	6	6	5	5	5	5	5	5	5
ROGERS	3	3	3	3	3	2	2	3	4	3	3
RODRIGUEZ	2	2	2	3	2	1	0	1	1	1	0
THORPE	1	1	1	1	0	0	0	1	1	1	2
NICKLAUS	2	2	1	1	2	3	2	2	3	3	3
CRENSHAW	2	2	2	2	2	2	2	1	1	2	1
CONNER	1	0	0	1	0	1	1	0	0	1	
COOK J	1	1	1	1	1	1	1	1	1		
SCHROEDER J	2	2	1	1	0	0	0	0	1		

81st. U.S. OPEN CHAM

The Game

Why and how is par assigned to a hole?

Par is the score that an expert golfer should make on that particular hole; it is set in order to have a standard against which to measure score and determine handicaps. Par is generally based on the length of the hole, but allowances are made for level of difficulty caused by terrain features. The USGA's guidelines for par according to distance are:

Par	Men	Women
3	up to 250	up to 210
4	251 to 470	211 to 400
5	over 470	401 to 575

Why is four the accepted number of golfers for one group?

In its earliest form, golf was strictly match play in format, and four.is the smallest number of players for team matches. As a result, competition between clubs in England and America in the nineteenth century was always in the foursome grouping. Even as the format changed, however, numbers greater than four were generally frowned upon because they slowed down the game and caused confusion around the green.

The Game

Why is it considered bad form to walk across someone's line before he or she putts?

There are two main reasons why this breach of etiquette is considered serious. Firstly, by walking on someone's line you may leave an indentation that could affect the roll of the putt. Secondly, the intrusion across a player's line may cause a break in the player's concentration. Most good players try to visualize the line of the putt as they are sizing it up. Walking across that line disturbs that visual picture.

In the early days of golf, why were feathers used as stuffing for golf balls?

The old "featheries" were surprisingly alive. A large amount of chicken feathers were boiled and then stuffed firmly into a leather cover. When the feathers dried and expanded they stretched the leather so it became quite resilient. The ball actually went a good distance, with drives of over 300 yards recorded, but the ball was phased out about 1850.

The Game

Why is a game of golf referred to as a "round"?

In the early days of golf, all courses were constructed in a circular fashion. The first hole was near the clubhouse, and the other holes would circle through the countryside, coming back to the starting point on the eighteenth hole.

Why is the word "divot" used to describe a piece of earth dislodged by a club stroke?

"Divot" is a Scottish word for a piece of turf.

The Game

Why is the tradition of "having the honor"—allowing the player who scored the lowest on the previous hole to tee off first—used, and what, if any, advantage does it bestow?

Having the honor is part of the rules, establishing a uniform system of order for playing first off the tee. To hit first can be a distinct advantage, as a good shot may put pressure on an opponent.

The Game

Why is the overlapping grip sometimes called the "Vardon"?

Harry Vardon, who won the British Open six times and the U.S. Open once, was a great promoter and golfer at the turn of the century. He was often photographed using the overlap grip. He is not, however, considered to be the inventor of the grip, as several well-known players, including Leslie Balfour Melville and J.H. Taylor, had used the grip successfully before Vardon reached fame as a golfer.

Why is the higher side of a cup on an incline called "the pro side"?

A good player will read the break of a putt correctly, allowing enough break and putting to the higher side. The lower side of the hole is sometimes called "the sucker's side" because the poor golfer will not read the break correctly.

The Game

Why are golf courses sometimes called "links"?

According to Webster Evans's *Encyclopedia of Golf* the word is derived from Old English *hlinc*, meaning ridge of land. Links land is gently undulating land, often running along the seashore. In the strict sense of the term, a links golf course should be one that borders the sea.

Why is a golfer who averages par referred to as a "scratch" player?

The Standard Scratch and Handicapping Scheme developed by the Council of National Golf Unions devised a system of comparing golf courses based on length. The score that was deemed its true par (much as courses are rated today) was called the "scratch score." A player who averaged scratch score was called a scratch man.

The Game

Why is "nassau" used to describe a match played on both nines and an overall eighteen?

A nassau bet sets up three separate matches: the front nine, the back nine and the entire eighteen holes. When a player or side goes down by two holes, a "press" can be made. A press doubles the amount of the bet and creates a new match for the number of holes remaining. This popular form of match comes from a betting practice that was very popular in the Caribbean Islands. The practice spread to the United States where it has become a standard form of betting in most clubs.

Why is the term "dormie" used when someone is ahead by the same number of holes left in the match?

"Dormie" probably comes from the Latin *dormire* "to sleep." "The player who is ahead cannot lose though he go to sleep."

The Game

Why is the word "putt" used in golf?

Putt comes from the word "put." Once on the green, the object of that particular stroke is to "put" the ball into the hole.

The Game

Why has golf become so popular?

It is estimated that there are over twenty million golfers in the United States alone, with a growth rate that will add one to two million golfers per year over the next ten years. Sixty percent of new golfers are women. There are several reasons for the boom. The baby boom generation, now at middle age, has found golf to be a recreation of the successful business executive. According to the National Golf Foundation 67 percent of business executives play the game; it is more than a cliche that many business transactions take place on a golf course. Compared to other adult games, golf offers many unique characteristics. As all holes and courses are different, the player is constantly faced with unique situations that require strategic decisions that are relatively scarce in other sports. The game is very difficult to master and offers a real challenge, appealing to many success-oriented people. The Japanese, who have a long history of being fascinated by very challenging games such as Go and the martial arts, have been taking up the game of golf in huge numbers despite the lack of courses. Several million golfers in Japan may never play on a real course, accepting golf's challenge solely on the driving range.

The game does not require size, strength or particularly outstanding athletic ability but emphasizes such attributes as tempo, concentration, strategy and accuracy. Combine the intrinsic elements of golf's lure with sunshine, fresh air and moderate exercise, and it becomes clear why the love affair has grown.

As A.A. Milne once said, "Golf is popular simply because it is the best game at which to be bad."

Why is the Ryder Cup match so named?

The Ryder Cup matches are played between American PGA professionals and pros from Europe every two years. An unofficial match between the U.S. and England played in Surrey, England, in 1926 prompted the tradition; the match was very popular and a wealthy seed merchant named Samuel Ryder presented a gold cup at the first official match at Worcester, Massachusetts, in 1927, with the American team winning.

The Game

Why is the term "bye" used when a player does not have an opponent in a match?

The term "bye" probably started as a farewell to someone who had lost a match 10 and 8 in an eighteen-hole match. Not having to play the remaining holes, an opponent in this situation also had a "bye," and gradually the term was extended to anyone who did not have to play a match.

Why does "fairway" describe the close-cut part of a course?

The Rules of Golf do not specifically define the word "fairway" but generally refer to it as "through the green." In early references to the game, the playing area was often called the "fair green." As time went on, the term "fairway," as opposed to the rough, became most common.

The Game

Why is the term "mulligan" used for the granting of a second chance at a drive on the first hole?

The origin of "mulligan" is not clear, but it may be rhyming slang for "have at it again."

Why is a very poor round of golf sometimes referred to as "military golf"?

A hacker having an extremely wild day off the tee calls to mind a drill sergeant's cadence call: "Left-right-left-right!"

Why is a "skins" competition so named?

In a "skins" game players compete on each hole, the player with the lowest score winning a "skin." The term goes back to the days when a hunter would display his success by the number of pelts or skins he had upon returning from the hunt.

The Game

Why is the phrase "rub of the green" used to describe any odd or accidental occurrence in the game of golf?

The 1812 code of the royal and Ancient Golf Committee used the following expression in Rule IX: "Whatever happens to a ball by accident must be reckoned a rub of the green." "Rub" here means a hindrance or difficulty (as in the Elizabethan phrase "there's the rub"), and "green" is a common term for the whole course.

Why is the word "stymie" used in golf?

The word "stymie" comes from the Scottish word *styme*, meaning a person who is partially blind. In golf, stymie rules used to allow a golfer to putt his ball onto the line of his opponent in order to block the path to the hole. If you were stymied, you could not "see" the hole. Stymies were taken out of the Rules in 1952 as they tended to lessen the importance of true golfing skill and slow the game down. Today, "stymied" is used by golfers to describe a situation where they are blocked along their line to the green by an obstacle such as a tree or large rock.

The Game

Why do golfers tend to dress in very colorful attire?

The tradition of bright clothing goes back to the very beginnings of the game. Archers would wear bright red uniforms for much the same reason hunters wear orange and red today. As the early clubs were often made up of mostly military men, the idea of wearing bright clothing in order to be seen while playing carried over to the game of golf.

Why are double eagles rarer than holes in one?

On the 1987 PGA Tour there were thirty holes in one but only two double eagles. Holes in one are usually made on relatively short par-three holes. While certainly difficult, a hole in one is much easier than having to hit two very long and extremely accurate shots on a par five, the second of which, of course, goes into the hole.

The Game

Why do many instructional books equate an "average" golfer with a poor one?

Golf is a very difficult game to master. According to the National Golf Foundation, the average golfer will shoot in the high 90s on a par 72 course. Only one player in twelve will break eighty with any consistency. The practice, experience, knowledge and athletic ability needed to play golf is well beyond the level possible for the "average" golfer.

Why is the term "Grand Slam" used to describe winning the U.S. Open, British Open, PGA Championship and the Masters?

"Grand Slam," with its baseball meaning obviously in mind, was first used in golf to describe Bobby Jones's amazing feat in 1930 of winning the U.S. and British Opens and the national amateur championships of both countries. With the lessening in importance of amateur play, the phrase eventually arrived at its modern meaning.

The Game

Why is three under par on one hole sometimes referred to as an "albatross"?

"Albatross" is simply an extension of birdie and eagle and like them is considered an American term. The word never really caught on among golfers, however, and the term "double eagle" has generally replaced it in modern golf vernacular.

Why is the handicap system often used at amateur net tournaments called the "Callaway System"?

In 1957 Lionel F. Callaway invented a system that yields instant handicaps based on the round shot. The system is used extensively when large numbers of competitors who do not have handicaps play. The system eliminates the worst score of the round in descending order based on the total score for the day.

The Game

Why is the Walker Cup so named?

The Walker Cup matches are played between the top amateurs from the United States and Great Britain. The Cup began with an unofficial match the day before the British Amateur Championship in 1921. George H. Walker, president of the United States Golf Association, had agreed to provide a cup for the winning team starting in 1922. The newspapers quickly referred to it as the Walker Cup and the name stuck.

The Game

Why is the Curtis Cup so named?

The Curtis Cup matches are played between the top women amateurs from the United States and Great Britain every two years. An unofficial competition, begun in 1905 between the two countries, steadily grew in popularity until it was decided to begin an official event in 1932. Two sisters, Margaret and Harriet Curtis, had played in many of the unofficial matches and offered to donate a cup for the competition. The Curtis sisters had won four USGA Ladies' Championships between them at the time.

The Game

Why do golfers yell "fore!" to warn others of an approaching shot?

Most experts think the term derives from a warning used by the British Army in battle, which formed ranks of infantry at the front with artillery located to the rear. Before firing a volley, the artillery yelled "beware before" to the infantry, who then lay down to let the cannonballs fly overhead. Shortened to "fore," the term eventually came to be used by golfers to warn other players of a missile headed their way.

Why are there eighteen holes?

The number of holes on a golf course was not fixed until the eighteenth century. In 1764 the Royal and Ancient Golf Club reduced its number of holes from twenty-two to eighteen by combining eight of them into four. As legislation on the Rules was being written at the same time, eighteen was agreed upon by common consent.

The Game

Why is the term "caddy" used in golf, and what
is its history?

The word probably comes from the French word
cadet, meaning "young man." Mary Queen of Scots,
an avid golfer, used the young men of her court to
carry her clubs. The word had been adopted by the
Scottish to refer to a porter or someone who does odd
jobs, but partly because of Mary's use "caddy" was
gradually applied to the young men who did the
various jobs as greenskeeper, club repairer and ball-
marker around the course before narrowing in meaning
to its present use.

The Equipment

The evolution of golf equipment traces the game's history and chronicles the never-ending search for the perfect match between man and tool. Watch a golf junkie in a pro shop as he works his way through a rack of putters. Suddenly, he holds one in front of him as the thousand-yard stare tells us, "Yes, this is it! This is the one that will change my golfing life!" Men who cannot explain the function of a carburetor can explain how swingweight and torque are related in the shaft of a 2 iron.

From the early featheries to aerodynamically designed dimple patterns, golf-ball technology has evolved steadily. Clubs have gone from crude wooden sticks to finely crafted instruments of boron or titanium. Golfers of all ages engage in love affairs with their equipment in the search for the perfect tools.

The Equipment

Why does a golf ball have dimples?

The primary function of dimples is to provide lift. As the ball spins off the club, the tiny cups trap air in such a way that the air moves more quickly over the top of the ball than around the bottom, causing the ball to rise. This aerodynamic principle is the same as the one that causes airplanes to lift off the ground.

The Equipment

Why does a golf club have grooves?

The grooves on a club stop the ball from sliding up the clubface at impact. As a ball is struck, it will ride up on the clubface until the grooves and dimples of the ball interact to trap the ball and help propel it forward.

Why do some putters have grips that are flat on the top?

Under the Rules of Golf (4-1c) putters are the only clubs that can have such grips. The purpose of the flat grip is to accommodate the most common putting grip, which places both thumbs directly down the middle of the shaft. This grip helps prevent the hands from rolling and thus throwing the ball off line.

The Equipment

Why are wood clubs rounded on the face instead of flat from heel to toe?

This feature is called "bulge." The slight curve from heel to toe actually helps shots that are mishit. A ball struck on the toe, for example, will fly off to the right, but the bulge on the clubface will give it a counterclockwise spin, causing it to hook back toward the center of the fairway. A ball struck on the heel will react in the opposite manner.

Why are the spikes on golf shoes so arranged?

The proper golf swing requires that a golfer maintain good balance while shifting weight from one foot to the other. The spikes on most golf shoes are placed so that they line the outsides of both the heel and sole areas. This design allows the golfer to push off the back foot on the downswing, with his front foot receiving the weight transfer without slipping forward at impact and beyond.

The Equipment

Why aren't golf balls numbered higher—such as 9, 10 or 11?

In the late fifties and early sixties, several golf ball manufacturers did number balls into the double figures. Touring pros, out of superstition, tended to only use low-numbered balls, those numbered 1 through 3 in particular. The everyday golfer soon picked up on the practice and the manufacturers adjusted accordingly.

The Equipment

Why do golfers wear only one glove?

With most grips used today, the left hand (for righthanders) has far more contact with the club. In the Vardon overlapping grip, for example, the entire left hand is placed on the club, while only parts of the first three fingers of the right come into contact with it. While it affords better gripping action for the left hand, a glove would inhibit the function of the right, which is to "feel" and control the clubface.

Why do some wood clubs have a small bulge on the bottom of the club where the shaft ends?

If you are able to see the tip of the shaft on the bottom of the club then this is a "through-bore" club, in which the shaft penetrates all the way through to where the tip is exposed. If the tip is not exposed then the club is said to be a "blind bore." The design changes mainly deal with the flex characteristics of the type of shaft used. Through-bore models tend to handle stiff shaft characteristics better for most steel shafts, but the difference is minor as flex can be controlled by the shaft itself.

The Equipment

Why are some new clubs featuring "offset" as a game-improvement aid?

An offset club is one in which the clubface is set back from the hosel, a design feature that allows the golfer to set up for the shot with his hands in front of the ball and promotes a swing that hits down on the ball.

Why is a sand wedge designed differently from other clubs?

A sand wedge is specifically designed to slide under the ball through the sand. The back of the flange or bottom of the club is lower than the front or lead edge of the club. This design feature, called "bounce," allows the club to pass through the sand without becoming buried. In a sand shot, the clubface never actually touches the ball; the concussion of the club striking the sand actually causes the ball to fly up and out of the trap.

The Equipment

Why did wood clubs have tightly wound string around the neck of the club?

Called "whipping," the tightly wound twine served to reinforce the joint where the shaft meets the clubhead. Without this reinforcement the wood near the neck would crack and split from the force of the swing. Today, various materials are used instead of whipping to reinforce the joint.

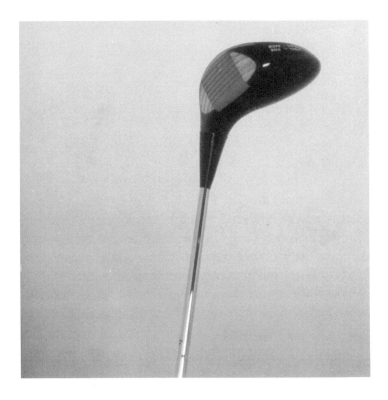

The Equipment

Why are some clubs curved on the bottom and
advertised as "radiused"?

"Radiused," "cambered" or "rocker-soled" clubs are
curved from heel to toe to enable the average golfer to
make more solid contact from various lies. With a
curved sole, only a small part of the leading edge of
the club comes into contact with the turf. A radiused
club is particularly advantageous for lies on hard pan,
or where fairways are dry and grass is sparse.

Why are some wood clubs said to be "persimmon"?

Persimmon is a term used for trees that belong to the
ebony family, which have fine, hard wood. In golf, a
persimmon wood is one that is made from a solid
block of wood. In contrast, a wood club made from
glueing layers of wood together is called "laminated."
Metal woods are sometimes referred to as "Pittsburgh
Persimmon."

The Equipment

Why have some manufacturers started using titanium in their shafts?

Titanium, famous for its use in aircrafts, is lighter than steel and has excellent properties of flex and torque. The lightness of titanium shafts creates a lower center of gravity. Because of this shift in weight, the club can be swung easily and still generate good clubhead speed because the new weighting characteristic keeps the "kick" in the shaft. The one notable drawback is expense, with a price tag of $240 per club in 1992 not uncommon.

Why are golf grips tapered from top to bottom when the grips of tennis rackets, fishing rods and baseball bats, for example, are either straight or tapered upwards?

There are several reasons for the shape of the golf grip. Firstly, the shaft of a golf club must taper from top to bottom to flex properly for the golf swing. Also, the golf grip places the two hands closely together so that the meat of the hands is at the top and the fingers at the bottom. Finally, the tapering of the grip allows greater freedom of wrist action, vital to the proper golf swing.

Why are manufacturers using metal in the construction of "woods"?

The metal woods offer the opportunity to create different weight characteristics that can help a golf game. Perimeter weighting, for example, placing weight around the perimeter of the clubface, reduces the amount of twisting at impact. This feature, theoretically, should cause off-center hits to fly straighter.

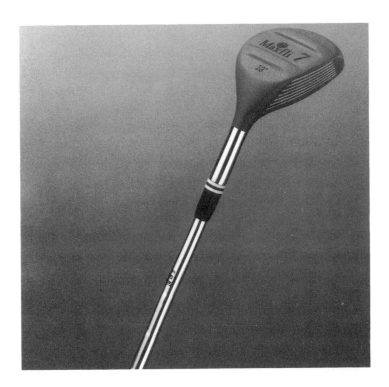

The Equipment

Why is the word "tee" used for the wooden peg that holds the ball?

The word "tee" probably comes from the Scottish *teay*, a small pile of sand. For many years golfers would make a pile of sand or dirt and place their ball on top of it for driving. In 1920 Dr. William Lowell, a Boston dentist, invented the wooden tee to prevent his hands from becoming scratched.

Why are the clubfaces of woods rounded from top to bottom?

It is mostly a matter of appearance and optics. The clubface is rounded from top to bottom to give the appearance of loft. If the face were cut straight from top to bottom, it would appear almost vertical to the golfer. By rounding, or creating "roll," golf manufacturers are actually helping golfers' confidence in getting the ball into the air.

The Equipment

Why were the earlier models of golf balls called "gutta-percha"?

"Gutta-percha" is a material tapped from several species of Malaysian trees. It resembles rubber but contains more resin and hardens when exposed to air. Golf legend has it that a professor at St. Andrews University received a statue of Vishnu packed in gutta-percha. An avid golfer, the professor rolled the material and tried it out as a golf ball. The ball did not fly very well at first, but as it became more roughed up it started to rise higher. The idea of dimples (to provide lift) thus came into being. Early golf ball craftsmen would place the dimples by hand; later molds were made to produce the early versions of the ball we use today.

The Equipment

Why are some clubs featuring "cavity back" designs?

"Cavity back" clubs are usually investment clubs with a hollowed-out area directly behind the hitting area. This design feature allows club-makers to place additional weight in the heel and toe areas and consequently help the golfer hit straighter shots from off-center hits.

The Equipment

Why do some club manufacturers refer to a "moment of inertia" in describing the characteristics of their clubs?

The moment of inertia is the measure of any object's inertial resistance to turning. The moment of inertia is related to weight and the distribution of weight of the object to be turned. In the clubface, a perimeter weighting or heel-toe weighting design will help prevent twisting by increasing the moment of inertia when shots are hit slightly off of the sweet spot.

Why do many golf ball companies feature such numbers as 382 and 384 on their balls?

The numbers refer to the number of dimples on the ball. The dimples are arranged in certain patterns to produce desired flight characteristics. For example, Maxli's DDH design is an arrangement of dimples in a dodecahedron pattern that promotes lift and carry in a stabilized flight.

The Equipment

Why do golf balls have compression ratings of 80, 90 and 100?

The compression ratings of 80 (soft), 90 (medium) and 100 (hard) measure the technical concept of "coefficient or restitution," which refers to a ball's ability to spring back into shape after being struck. Tests have shown that the higher the compression the farther the ball will go, regardless of the force of the swing. The soft and medium compression balls are favored by many players because they offer a better feel. Compression is measured by the tightness of the windings or the density of the material in the two-piece ball. Most women use an 80 compression; big hitters and top players use the 100; and the vast majority of all other golfers play with the 90.

The Equipment

Why are tees still made of wood instead of more durable materials?

Tees have been made of wood for over sixty years for several reasons. Firstly, tees made of metal and plastic can scratch and damage wood clubs. The cost of wooden tees has remained very low, and the supply is plentiful. Of course, as with most things in the game of golf, there is tradition. Many top players would never dream of playing with anything but a wooden tee, and the vast majority use white ones only.

Why were aluminum shafts phased out?

Aluminum proved to be too soft for golf shafts, unable to take the tremendous torque and flex involved in the golf swing. Players using aluminum in the late sixties found that the sound at impact was muffled and the distance off the tee quite reduced.

The Equipment

Why is the USGA's robot used for testing golf balls and clubs called "Iron Byron"?

Iron Byron was actually modeled after the swing of Byron Nelson. The USGA wanted a robot that would replicate a near-perfect golf swing based on the swing plane, arc and height of an average-sized man. Nelson's swing, considered to be a classic example of the proper golf swing, was used to set the baseline data for the robot to emulate.

The Equipment

Why, in the early days of golf, were clubs given names such as "niblick" and "mashie"?

Up until the first half of the twentieth century, golf clubs were sold individually. A golfer would look through a batch of mid-irons until he found the right mashie. As a marketing device, club manufacturers created matched sets of clubs. With the onset of matched sets, the system of numbering clubs came into use instead of individual names for each club.

Why were the knickers that golfers used to wear called "plus fours"?

In order to create the effect of pants bloused just below the knee, manufacturers added four inches to the normal length of short pants. Thus the length of the knickers was normal length plus four inches.

The Equipment

Why are Ping clubs so named?

Karsten Solheim, founder of Ping clubs and Karsten Manufacturing, made his first putter on his workbench. The putter was intended to be lightweight and feature heel- and toe-weighing. When Solheim tried it for the first time he was surprised to hear a rather pronounced *ping!* when he struck the putt. Thus the Ping was born. The first putter was not successful, but subsequent models made an impression on the touring pros and soon the business boomed.

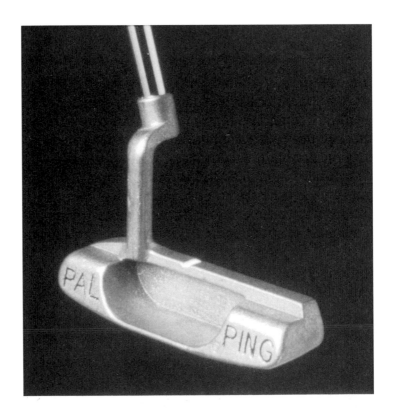

The Equipment

Why is the grain in persimmon woods important?

Most golf-club mavens look for a matching grain pattern through all the wood clubs as a sign of careful craftsmanship and matching stocks of wood.

Why were early clubs referred to as "spoons"?

In the early days of golf, clubs that are now called irons were made with spoonlike concave faces. The clubs had specific names such as the "long spoon," "mid-spoon" and "baffing spoon" depending on their use. With the advent of matched, numbered club sets, this term fell from use.

The Equipment

Why was there once a difference between the size of golf balls used in Great Britain and the U.S.?

The difference in size (U.S. 1.68 inches, G.B. 1.62) goes back to 1931, when American manufacturers began making balls slightly larger than the standard British ball. In 1931 the USGA approved the 1.68 diameter as the standard for golf competition. The Royal and Ancient Golf Committee did not go along with the change, and the two countries played with different-sized balls. In 1990, however, the ball was standardized at 1.68 throughout the world, as the R and A agreed to the new standard for play.

The Equipment

Why do grips come in different thicknesses?

The grip differences come in increments of 1/32 of an inch and may have an effect on the swing. Thicker grips tend to restrict wrist and hand action and can help to prevent hooking. On the other hand, thinner grips promote greater hand and wrist action and can help cure a slice.

Why is the term "swingweight" used? Why don't manufacturers just call it the weight of the club?

"Swingweight" is a measure of the club's weight distribution based on a balance point between the head and end of the grip. The overall weight of a club is called the static weight.

The Equipment

Why and how is a "Stimpmeter" used in golf?

A Stimpmeter is a grooved bar used to measure
the speed of greens. A ball is placed on the bar,
which is raised until the ball rolls freely. The distance that the ball rolls is measured and the opera-
tion is repeated several times, with an average
being taken. The speed of a green is important to
ensure consistency and to create conditions that
are considered to be of championship calibre.

Why do some manufacturers use beryllium copper
on clubheads?

Beryllium copper adds weight to the clubhead,
cuts down on glare and allows the grooves to be
cut more sharply into the clubface.

The Equipment

Why is a putter used from off the green called a "Texas wedge"?

Many players from Texas used this technique because of the tough wind conditions there. Using a putter keeps the shots low and the wind's influence minimal. Ben Hogan popularized the technique and the term in the 1950s.

The Equipment

Why do shafts come in different flexes?

Most club manufacturers make four flexes for
their shafts. Generally, the type of flex depends on
the amount of force exerted on the swing. A
powerful swing requires a shaft with little flex in
it, as the force of the swing would cause a whippy
shaft to bend too much so that the clubhead
would strike the ball too soon in the player's
swing. Additionally, the clubhead would twist as it
reached impact, causing a severe hook. On the
other hand, a player who swings easily needs a
more flexible shaft in order to have some "kick"
or benefit from the shaft bending as a result of
centrifugal force. The four standard flexes are:

    X-Stiff — Very powerful swing
    Stiff   — Strong player
    Regular — Normal swing, average player
    Soft   — Very slow swing

The Equipment

Why are some irons referred to as "muscle back"?

The term "muscle back" refers to forged irons that have bulges or ripples on the back of the clubhead opposite the hitting area. The muscle-back iron creates mass near the hitting zone, for additional power.

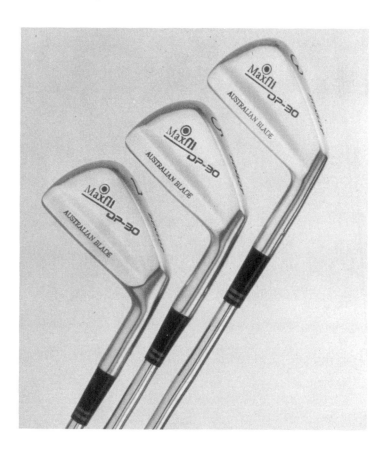

The Swing

None of man's movement has been more analyzed,
filmed, written about and debated than the golf swing.
The search for the perfect golf swing drives us to read
about such things as a "power arc" with the intensity
of a cardiologist reading an EKG. But the sad truth is
that while there are proven principles, there is no one
swing model that is absolute. On the PGA Tour we see
slow, smooth passes and swings that would cause
severe injury if emulated. We often accept advice and
try things that will bring us closer to our goal of
breaking 80...90... or simply getting into double figures
for the first time. Often we follow the advice without
knowing why. Golf is a mysterious game and the why
of how we swing is part of golf's most interesting lore.

The Swing

Why should the left arm remain straight during the swing?

At the moment of impact the left arm must be fully extended in order to let the hands come through in a smooth, powerful motion. During the backswing the left arm remains straight in order to maintain a smooth, wide arc for the swing. If the left elbow breaks down, extra motion is required to bring the clubface back to the intended plane. The result is a loss of power and accuracy.

Why is a slow takeaway important to a good swing?

Sam Snead once compared taking a club back to taking a hammer back to strike a nail. To really drive the nail you draw the hammer back slowly. The same principle holds true in the golf swing. A fast backswing makes it very difficult to control the position at the top of the swing and can throw the clubhead off the intended plane, causing a loop or other movement to get the clubhead back onto the proper path. A slow takeaway promotes a rhythm and tempo that is easier to control and repeat.

The Swing

Why is it so important to keep your head down during the swing?

It is not so much important to keep your head down as it is to keep it still. The head should be considered the hub of a wheel for your shoulders and arms, creating a center for the arc and plane of the swing. If your head bobs up or down, a top or fat shot can result. If your head moves backward or forward, the plane of the swing can be altered, causing a push or pull with the ball flying left or right of the intended path.

The Swing

Why are many chips stubbed or hit fat?

The most common cause of a stubbed chip shot is being too wristy. A player who uses his or her hands to direct the force and path of the clubhead takes a strong chance of hitting behind the ball. The best way to avoid this problem is to keep a firm left wrist and use a pendulum-type swing that is made with the arms. Many top players use the reverse overlap putting grip and a putting stroke to create the desired effect. Strike the ball as you would a putt and let the natural loft of the club get the ball into the air.

The Swing

Why are most putts missed?

Many professionals believe that the main cause of the missed putt is the mishit. A mishit occurs when the ball is struck inside or outside the sweet spot on the putter's face. A second cause is mis-alignment, in which the putter face is slightly open or slightly closed at the address. Errors in judging the amount of break and the strength required are also key in making a successful putt. Finally, there is the uncontrollable factor of the green itself. Grass texture and tiny bumps may contribute more to missed putts than we generally think. In *The Search for the Perfect Swing*, Alastair Cochran and John Stobbs tell of a putting machine set up to make putts perfect in alignment and speed. At twenty feet the machine could only make 50 percent of its putts because of inconsistencies in the green.

The Swing

Why do shanks occur?

The shanked shot is one in which the ball strikes the hosel on the inside part of the clubface. The ball shoots out to the right at almost a 90-degree angle from your target line. Generally, the shank is caused by one of two things: 1) taking the club to the inside too quickly and either coming back into the ball at a sharp angle from the inside or looping the club to the outside and cutting back to the ball at an angle; or 2) poor balance in which you move onto your toes at impact. Shanks often occur when the ball lies below your feet.

Cure the shank by being careful during the takeaway, ensuring that the clubface goes straight back from the ball instead of being jerked to the inside. Set your weight on the insides of your feet and keep the head as still as possible during the swing.

Why do hooks run when they land, while fades tend to stop more quickly?

A hooked or drawn shot is generally produced by a closed clubface, a fade or slice by an opened one. An opened face creates more loft and thus a higher shot with more backspin. The closed-face shot tends to fly lower and have less backspin.

The Swing

Why are touring pros so accurate and weekend players so dismal in hitting wedge shots to the green?

There are several reasons for this pattern. Mainly, the touring pros use a different type of swing for the wedge as opposed to the other clubs. Weekend players tend to take the club back in the one-piece motion and wide arc that is fine for most full shots. The touring pro uses a backswing that is wristy and upright and a sharp descending downswing that pinches the ball out of the turf. The pro also keeps leg movement to a minimum and lets the hands and arms swing the club for greater accuracy.

The Swing

Why is a grip said to be "weak" or "strong"?

These terms refer to the amount of hand action
produced by the placement of the left or leading
hand on the club. In a weak grip, the left hand is
turned toward the left with the V in the hand
pointing toward the left shoulder. A weak grip
prevents the right hand from rolling over to close
the face of the club and causes a hooked shot. A
strong grip is just the opposite: the hands are
turned toward the right, allowing a free and
powerful hand action that promotes a hook. Most
pros advocate a neutral grip that has the Vs pointing to the cheeks.

The Swing

Why is it that many players fail to improve their swings despite much practice?

Many players confuse hitting balls with practice. If you watch golfers at a crowded driving range you will see many who are hitting ball after ball with the same club (usually a driver) without ever checking their grip, stance or alignment. Every shot in practice should be hit at a target with concentration on the fundamentals and an evaluation of the result.

Why do many top players place their left index finger over the fingers of their right hand when putting?

This putting grip is called the reverse-overlap grip. By placing the left finger over the fingers of the right, the hands tend to work as a one-piece unit. If the hands are spread apart on the shaft, as in a baseball grip, the putting stroke becomes wristy. A wristy stroke is unpredictable and more difficult to control. Most top players try to use a pendulum-type putting stroke in which the swinging action is originated in the larger muscles of the arms and shoulders.

The Swing

Why do many top players use a waggle or slight
movement before they start the backswing?

Basically there are two reasons for the movements
that precede the backswing. Firstly, the small
movements such as drawing the club back slightly
from the ball, serves as a mini-rehearsal for the
actual path of the backswing. These movements
also serve to break the tension of holding a club
stationary. The other slight movements, such as
moving the hands forward or bending the right
knee forward just prior to the backswing, are
often referred to as a "forward press." The forward press is a small movement in the opposite
direction of the backswing that helps prevent a
jerky motion in starting the club back from a
standing position. In earlier days, the forward
press was much more pronounced; the modern
swing has greatly reduced this movement to only a
slight move, which breaks inertia just before the
club is drawn back.

The Swing

Why is it common to hit "fliers," shots that sail with little backspin on them, from the rough?

In heavy rough the grass directly behind the ball becomes trapped between the ball and clubface at impact. The grass prevents the grooves of the clubface from grabbing the ball, so it tends to fly like a knuckleball through the air. It is best to take one less club and use a sharp descending downswing to snap the ball out with a minimum of interference from the grass. The ball will run farther, compensating for the change.

The Swing

Why have so many golfers bought golf instructional videos?

It is estimated that 90 percent of all American homes will have VCRs in the near future. This technology is well suited for golf instruction for several reasons. Because of the tremendous impact of television, Americans are increasingly becoming visual learners: they absorb and retain video material more readily than what they read or hear. Psychologists have discovered that many people are able to copy a particular athletic movement after watching filmed demonstrations. Golf videos enable many golfers to study the golf swings of the greats up close; they can emulate these swings in practice. Many golfers have found that watching videos just prior to playing helps with tempo and implants an overall swingthought for the proper golf swing.

The Swing

Why do golfers look at the ball rather than the hole when putting?

In almost every other sport that requires accuracy in propelling a missile (throwing a baseball, football, horseshoes, bowling, basketball, etc.), a player looks at the target rather than the ball or object being thrown or propelled. The main difference between these sports and golf is that a golf ball is being moved from a still position that is not in contact with any part of the player's body or equipment before the propelling action. When putting, the head must remain still so the body will not push or pull the ball off line. Many players have tried looking at the hole instead of the cup and report very good results for a short time. Johnny Miller putted by looking at the hole for a season or two on the Tour. The technique seems to work for a short time because the golfer has to increase his concentration with the new technique, and looking at the hole helps keep the head still. It tends to fade in effectiveness over time, as the concentration level wanes and the player becomes comfortable with the technique.

The Swing

Why is the downhill-sidehill shot so difficult?

There are two main reasons why this is a difficult
shot for the average golfer: 1) gravity and 2) lack
of practice. The golf swing requires proper
balance and a shifting of weight from the back to
the front foot on the downswing. By setting up on
a downhill-sidehill lie, you are pulled by gravity in
a way that seriously affects your balance and
swing plane. The key to overcoming this situation
is to reverse the effects of gravity. By bending
your knees more, standing more upright and
keeping your weight on the back foot as you set
up, you are creating a stance that compensates for
gravity. The second cause of difficulty for the
average golfer is lack of practice in this situation.
These tough lies are not as much fun to practice
as hitting drives off a tee, so most golfers avoid
them. The best advice is to find a spot that simu-
lates a severe downhill-sidehill situation and hit
balls until you gain confidence and a good sense
of technique and feel for the shot.

The Swing

Why is it important to keep your head over the ball while putting?

Keeping your head over the ball gets your eyes over the ball and along the target line. In doing this, you can move the putter back and forth along the target line and strike the ball along the intended path. If your head is back from the target line, you get a distorted view of how the putter is swung back and through.

The Swing

Why does wind cause so many problems for the average golfer?

As a golf ball only weighs 1.62 ounces the wind can play a significant role in the flight of a golf shot. Because the wind can affect a ball greatly, many golfers change their swings and tactics to a point where they become self-defeating. Generally, a golfer is better off swinging more slowly in the wind rather than speeding up. Teeing the ball low can cause a lower flight, but many times it only makes the tee shot more difficult to hit. Tee the ball only slightly lower than normal and concentrate on good contact. In club selection, the rule of thumb is to take one more club than is normally needed for every ten miles-per-hour of wind against and one club less for every ten miles-per-hour of wind behind you.

The Swing

Why are the long irons so difficult to hit?

There are several reasons why the long irons
present problems. First, they have long shafts and
little loft. These clubs require a long, full backswing and a smooth, sweeping motion down and
through the ball. Most high handicappers run into
problems with the long irons because they swing
too hard in an attempt to gain distance, disrupting
the swing plane. The long irons will provide
distance if struck solidly with a smooth swing.

Why do some golfers tee the ball high, then tilt
the tee and ball backward as far as possible?

The idea behind this maneuver is to create lift.
The driver has a very shallow face (about 12
degrees of loft) and is meant to strike the ball on
a slightly upward swing path. Teeing the ball on a
slight slant gives the impression of hitting at a ball
that is set to lift off. While the effect of this type
of tee is probably psychological at best, many
players feel it is a helpful technique.

The Swing

Why is it that many players hit great shots at a
driving range but cannot bring the same shots to
the golf course?

There are two possible explanations for this
common complaint: tension and self-correction.
At the driving range, the golfer is relatively free of
tension. Tension restricts the swing and speeds up
tempo. On the golf course with your Sunday foursome, tension is present in every shot whether or
not you are aware of it. Secondly, at a driving
range you might hit ten 5-irons in a row. As you
hit each one you make subtle corrections and gain
a feel for the shot. On the golf course, you might
hit two 5-irons all day—both in isolated instances
under pressure. The key is to develop muscle
memory, reduce tension and trust your swing.

The Swing

Why are trap shots so difficult?

Actually, the trap shot is not too difficult for players who know how to execute it. Most golfers do not practice this shot and use the wrong technique to get the ball out of a trap. Too often, the average golfer tries to scoop the ball out by using a wide arc and extra motion at impact to lift the ball up and out. The proper method is to make a slow smooth backswing that is very upright and a sharp descending downswing that cuts into the sand about two inches behind the ball. The club should pass under the ball and the swing should be completed with a high finish.

The Swing

Why is one of golf's most common faults called a "reverse pivot" and what exactly is it?

The reverse pivot comes from shifting weight to the back foot during the downswing. In the proper golf swing, the hips should slide forward at the top of the swing and the weight should shift to the front foot. In the reverse pivot a player shifts to the back foot in an attempt to get more power or to scoop the ball into the air. The reverse pivot usually produces topped shots that dribble along the ground. Many golfers who played baseball as youngsters have a tendency to shift to the back foot as is taught in the baseball swing. But the power of a golf swing comes from centrifugal force; the power of a baseball swing comes from the arms and hands.

The Swing

Why is it that many top golfers seldom take practice swings, but take several when making a wedge shot?

Many top players do not take full practice swings because they have honed their swings through practice and know exactly how the full swing feels. By eliminating practice swings they conserve energy. However, when faced with a short pitch or chip, many top players do take rehearsal swings. Distance on short shots is determined and regulated by the length of the backswing. The good players take a series of swings until they find the length of the backswing required for the upcoming shot. With the proper amount of backswing in their muscle memory they now have a good sense of the shot.

The Swing

Why is it that most beginners start out slicing instead of hooking?

There are two main reasons for this pattern: grip and swing plane. Most people who grip a golf club for the first time hold it so that the left hand is turned to the right, a very natural way to hold a club and the preferred method for gripping a baseball bat. However, in golf the wrists turn or pronate and do not break as in baseball. The incorrect grip leaves the face of the club open, and the ball flies off with sidespin. The beginner also has a tendency to hit the ball from the outside, which produces a sidespin as well. The inside-out swing plane seems counterproductive to the raw beginner, who is slicing the ball to the right anyway.

The Swing

Why is shoulder-turn so important to a good swing?

Full shoulder-turn during the swing creates a wider arc. The wider the arc, the longer the clubhead will travel and thus build up speed. Clubhead speed, of course, translates into distance, but a good shoulder-turn may also help accuracy. In returning the clubhead to the ball it is easier to control the large muscle groups involved in a turn than it is to control the wrists and hands. The good player allows the big muscle groups to control and drive the swing and the hands and arms to transmit the power.

The Swing

Why is it difficult to judge distances on desert courses?

In general, desert courses have few trees and are very flat from tee to green. Without these terrain features, gaining a perspective is difficult. As you look at a distant point, your mind and eye compute distance by the relative size of objects near that point. Telephone poles along a highway, for example, help us determine distance by the apparent size. Many top players use their knowledge of distance to their advantage by visualizing how far they can hit a 9-iron, then how far for an 8 and so on until they gauge the right club to cover the distance to the pin rather than relying on estimation.

The Pros

In the 1920s country clubs began to spread across the country. In the winter months, the club pros headed to Florida and, naturally, competitions sprang up. Gradually, these competitions spread into Georgia and the Carolinas as the pros headed north in the spring. In this way the beginnings of the Tour were formed. While famous amateurs Francis Ouimet and Bobby Jones had dominated the golfing public's attention for years, new names such as Sarazen, Hagen, Hogan, Nelson and Snead swept across the nation in the Thirties, Forties and Fifties. The charisma of Arnold Palmer and televised tournaments brought the general public to the game and set the foundation for the tremendous boom in the game today.

The PGA and LPGA Tours are followed by hundreds of thousands of fans with deep interest and dedication. They watch in quiet flocks called galleries, carry no banners, applaud all competitors and never pull against anyone. The golf gallery empathizes with the competitors in a way that is seldom matched in any other sport. Most of us will never know what it is like to look at a Roger Clemens fastball or to trap-block Howie Long. Yet each member of the gallery knows exactly what it feels like to have a five-foot downhill curler for a needed par.

The pros are the epitome of mastery. We copy their mannerisms, use their equipment, wear their clothes and try to swing their swings. The glamour and mastery of the professionals offer more than just heroes to emulate, they represent the state of the art for millions of would-be artists.

The Professionals

Why don't players on the professional tour concede holes or putts in sudden-death playoffs when the hole is obviously lost?

Most of the PGA tournaments are medal play and require that all holes be completed. If a tournament goes into a playoff, it does not automatically become a match-play event.

Why did tournaments stop paying appearance fees to the top pros?

The PGA outlawed the practice of paying appearance fees because several agencies gained too much power by having many big-name players in their stables. Such an agency could make or break a tournament just by the number of big names that they could promise or withhold. The PGA prohibited the practice in order to bring stability for tournament committees, television and the fans.

The Professionals

Why do touring pros have such large bags?

Besides being moving billboards for golf equipment manufacturers, the golf bags must carry many items to meet contingencies. A typical staff bag might carry the following: twenty-four golf balls, tees, six gloves (pros change them about every six holes), a sweater, a rainsuit, a rain hood to protect the clubs, an extra pair of golf shoes and socks (in case of wet or very humid weather), an extra towel, an umbrella, spikes and a spike wrench, a yardage book, a rules book, coins, sunscreen, Band-aids, pencils and fruit (for snacks).

The Professionals

Why do touring pros sometimes look into the cup while sizing up a putt?

They are not looking into the cup but at the rim around it. If the grass is clipped very closely on one side of the cup it may indicate that a putt will break in the opposite direction. As the mower passed over the cup it clipped the grass on the higher part more closely. Also, they inspect the rim to see if it has become broken or worn. If the rim is worn they may have to hit a putt that "dies" at the hole rather than a firm putt that might spin out.

Why do many pros carry three wedges in their bags?

The third wedge added to the pitching and sand wedges is a club with an extremely high degree of loft, ranging up to about 65 degrees. This wedge is used for finesse shots of under 50 yards where the pro needs to pop the ball over a bunker or water and make it stop quickly. The club comes in handy as well for shots over trees, off hard pan and on steep downhill lies near the green. Many pros take the 3-iron out of the bag to make room for the third wedge.

The Professionals

Why do touring pros tend to walk by themselves
in tournaments and not talk much with fellow
competitors or the gallery during a round?

It is not because they are unfriendly. The pros
need to concentrate on the strategy required for
the upcoming shot and do not want to become
distracted. Secondly, under the Rules of Golf,
they may not receive advice or assistance from
anyone except their caddies. Should they accidentally discuss such things as club selection or course
condition they may face a penalty. There are also
penalties for slow play that each player must be
aware of as he or she plays a round.

Why do touring pros sometimes look straight up
when they are selecting a club?

Some may be praying. Most likely, however, the
pros are looking at the tops of the trees. The
winds at the tree-top level will have a far more
pronounced effect on their shots than the wind at
ground level.

The Professionals

Why are purses so large today compared to a relatively short time ago?

At one time golf was considered to be the pastime of the rich. Since World War II the middle class has taken to golf in a continuous period of growth. Professional golf moved into the period of big paydays in the 1960s, when television began to tap into the growing interest in the game. At that time, the charismatic Arnold Palmer was the reigning king of golf whose good looks and daring play brought thousands of spectators to tournaments and sponsors to television. With Jack Nicklaus's brilliant play, Lee Trevino's color and Gary Player's power, personalities soon emerged as drawing cards. Corporate sponsors are well aware that the golfing fan is a good consumer and thus have been eager to have their names associated with golf's elite. While golf's ratings may be lower than other sporting events on television, the golf viewer is a prized consumer, as evidenced by the types of products advertised and the amount of money put out to attract the big names in golf.

The Professionals

Why do touring pros have to keep their own score?

The nature of the game demands that the "honor system" be used. In golf, the player himself may frequently be the only one aware of a rules infraction. For example, a player may be the only one to see any of the following infractions: a ball moves slightly after address; a new ball is put into play; a club is grounded slightly in a hazard; or a ball is struck twice during a swing. Most pros hold the integrity of the game in high regard and will call penalties on themselves without hesitation.

Why don't touring pros pick their own balls out of the cup after making a long putt?

To avoid creating additional spike marks near the hole, the pros have their caddies, who usually wear sneakers, retrieve the ball from the hole.

The Professionals

Why is the PGA Tour considered one of the most difficult major league sports to enter?

To qualify for a spot on the PGA golfers must play well over a period of elimination rounds against the best players in the world. The players on tour who finish between 1 and 125 on the annual money list are exempt from qualifying. Players who finish 126 to 150 must qualify at a 108-hole tournament in December. For players seeking to break into the Tour, qualification begins in early fall with a 72-hole tournament followed by a second elimination tournament of 72 holes. The initial field of 1,750 is cut down to 155 players who join the twenty-five touring pros for the December tournament to select the fifty players who will receive tour cards for the coming year. The 108-hole tournament is a pressure-packed event where a bad hole might mean a year's plans down the drain.

The Professionals

Why do touring pros change balls every few holes?

Golf balls tend to get out of round after being hit several times. The pros change balls to prevent having to putt with a ball that is out of round and would not roll in a true manner.

When sizing up a putt, why do touring pros look at the edge of the green, even if their ball is nowhere near it?

The pros often look for places where water has run off the green. The flow of water from a green may assist them in judging slopes and breaks otherwise indiscernible.

The Professionals

Why do pros on the tour often practice after their round?

Many pros say they practice after a round for two reasons—they played well or they played poorly. If they have played very well they like to keep hitting balls in order to keep the good tempo and rhythm going and get it into their muscle memory. On the other hand, if they have been having trouble with a particular part of their game, say driving, they will hit balls until they feel that they have worked out the problem and their confidence has returned.

The Professionals

Why do touring pros dread wet conditions the most?

The pros do not like wet conditions because reaction of the ball is unpredictable. The grooves on the irons become filled with water and reduce spin on the ball, which causes a knuckleball effect called a "flyer." This effect has the pros guessing at how far the ball will fly and how it will react upon hitting the green.

The Professionals

Why do touring pros write something on their golf balls before playing?

The pros are marking their balls for identification purposes. Because many pros use the same brand of golf balls, they place a few dots or circles on the ball to guard against mix-ups.

Why do touring pros count their clubs on the first tee?

The Rules of Golf allow only fourteen clubs during play. The pros often swap clubs and try new clubs on the practice tee as they warm up for a round, and it is not uncommon for a stray club to wind up in a pro's bag accidentally.

The Professionals

Why did the PGA Championship change from
match to stroke play?

In a word, television. A match play event is very
difficult to follow in a television format, with
some seventy-two pairings on the first day and the
chance that the stars will not be available for
action on air time. In a round-robin system,
players are eliminated until there are only two left
for the championship round. The championship
takes place on Sunday afternoon, and the cameras
have to follow only two players for over four
hours. The PGA decided that in order to
accommodate the television audience, a stroke
event would be more entertaining and profitable.

The Professionals

Why do the touring pros work their feet so deeply into the sand when they are in a bunker?

There are two reasons for this maneuver: by sinking their feet into the sand they anchor and prevent slipping while taking a swing; it is also the only legal way to test the consistency of the sand within the Rules of Golf.

Why do the touring pros sometimes walk up to the flagstick, pull it out and then put it back in before making a chip shot?

They want to ascertain if the pin is leaning in any direction. Sometimes a caddy will not place it all the way into the liner hole in the cup. When this happens the pin may lean against the player's line and keep a ball from dropping. The player may also be testing the rigidity of the pin. If the pin is very rigid, and the chip is makeable, the pro will probably remove the pin.

The Professionals

Why is Al Geiberger called "Mr. 59"?

Al Geiberger has won ten PGA Tour events including the 1966 PGA Championship, but he will forever be known for shooting the lowest score in a PGA event to date, a 59 in the second round of the Danny Thomas Memphis Classic in 1977. Geiberger's business card opens to a replica of the Colonial Club's scoreboard and the hole-by-hole tally of his OUT 29–IN 30–59.

Why do so many pros on the Tour wear a hat with the name "Amana" printed on it?

Amana Refrigeration, Inc., gave a free life insurance policy to the pros who wore it.

The Professionals

Why do many touring pros stand directly behind
the ball before taking their address?

The pros are sighting down the target line by
lining up the ball with the spot where they want it
to land. Many pick an intermediate target as well,
a leaf, divot or discolored patch of grass a few
feet in front of the ball and along the target line.
When they take the address position they line up
their feet, hips and shoulders along the line
created by the ball and the intermediate target a
few feet away.

Why don't the touring pros use yellow or orange
balls?

The colored balls are primarily intended for those
golfers who have difficulty finding their balls. The
touring pros have little problem with lost balls.
Additionally, the pros have spent a lifetime practicing with white golf balls, and many find the
change to bright colors distracting.

The Professionals

Why do many PGA tournaments feature Pro-Am tournaments as a prelude to the actual event?

Money—the Pro-Am tournaments make up a large percentage of the prize money offered at each tournament. Entry fees for an amateur in these tournaments easily run into the $1500-$3000 range. Multiply that entry fee by 300 to 400 amateurs and the value of such events can be readily appreciated. Many corporations use the Pro-Ams as perks for deserving executives and enticements for prospective customers. There are long waiting lists for the chance to play in some of the more prestigious tourneys such as the Bob Hope Desert Classic or the Dinah Shore. The invitation list to some of these events reads like a Who's Who of the Rich and Famous.

The Professionals

Why do touring pros always finish their preround
practice by hitting some soft wedge shots?

The pros like to finish their warm-up practice by
hitting soft wedge shots because the practice
promotes "feel" and develops the smooth rhythm
that they want to bring to the first tee.

Why are the pros on the bottom of a tournament
scoreboard called the "dawn patrol"?

The pairings for a tournament are done by score,
with the leaders teeing off last on the final two
days of the tournament. Thus, players at the
bottom, or those who just made the cut, must tee
off very early in the morning.

The Professionals

Why is it said that "you drive for show but putt for dough"?

It is felt that good putting is more important to winning money on the Tour. Statistics generally support this axiom. In 1987 Curtis Strange, the Tour's leading money-winner with $925,941, was 107th in driving distance (260.6 yards) but sixteenth in putting with 1.77 putts per hole. Ben Crenshaw ($638,194) was eighty-sixth in driving but first in putting. The Tour's long-drive champion for a year has never won a tournament in the year that he held the distinction since Tour records have been kept.

The Professionals

Why are cameras banned at many Tour events?

The pros are used to most normal crowd noises, but the anticipation of a camera click is very disconcerting to the players during actual play.

Why are the pros surveyed just before teeing off on the first and last days of a tournamemt?

The surveys are conducted by several independent market research companies who sell their information to the golf industry. Golf ball manufacturers, for example, use this information in their advertisements. Market research has shown that the golfing public, very conscious of the equipment and clothing used by the top professionals, make purchases (over a billion dollars in 1987) according to what is hot on the Tour. As an example, when Jack Nicklaus won the 1986 Masters using an oversized putter, McGregor was immediately overwhelmed with orders for it.

The Professionals

Why do touring pros mark their ball and lift it when it is a very simple putt?

They mark it to clean it of any grass or sand that may have clung to the ball on the prior putt. In addition, they also check to see if the ball is resting in a spike mark or ball divot, which might affect the roll of the ball after impact. This procedure may seem tedious to the average golfer, but the amount of money involved is considerable and the pros do not want to leave anything to chance.

Why do touring pros have brand names displayed on everything possible?

Touring pros receive all of their equipment and clothes free from the manufacturers. In addition, they receive cash bonuses for appearing on television and finishing high or winning a tournament. Some golf ball companies pay up to $12,000 for a win, some club manufacturers up to $20,000.

The Professionals

Why don't the men pros wear shorts on very hot days?

The PGA Tour has strict guidelines from everything from abusive language to appearance. In the appearance category shorts are forbidden. It is felt that full-length golf pants are more in keeping with the Tour's image of gentlemen playing a gentleman's game.

Why must an aspiring touring pro provide his financial statement to the PGA Tour before he is eligible to play?

The PGA wants to ensure that the pro has the financial ability to stay on the tour for the year. Traveling expenses, entrance fees, caddies and living expenses may run over $20,000 a year following the sun on the PGA Tour. The PGA officials do not want no-shows or open slots at a tournament because a pro could not afford the trip.

Why is the LPGA's Hall of Fame considered to be one of the toughest in all of sport?

The LPGA Hall of Fame has exacting criteria for admittance compared to the election format used in other sports. To be admitted to the LPGA Hall of Fame, a woman has to win thirty victories on the tour, including two different majors; thirty-five victories with one major; or forty victories without a win in a major.

The Professionals

Why do some touring pros have their caddies read their putts?

Most touring pros read their putts alone. Some have their caddies give their opinions on the speed and break, and others use their caddies as sounding boards, explaining the putt as they think out loud.

Why do pros on the Senior Tour wear a clip on their belts?

The money clip that the seniors wear has the Senior Tour logo on it and serves as identification that the player is eligible to play in Senior Tour events.

Why do pros hold their putters in front of their eyes when lining up a putt? Just what are they looking for?

This technique is called "plumb-bobbing." The purpose of plumbing is to help determine slope. By holding the putter perpendicular to the hole, the player can see if the cup is tilted, a clear indication of slope.

Why do many pros insist that their caddies carry the golf balls in their pockets?

This practice is called "warming the eggs." Many pros believe that warming the golf balls help them to fly farther. While warming does enhance the elasticity of the ball, it would require illegal means to raise the temperature of the ball to get any significant benefits from it.

The Professionals

Why do many pros stare at their coin before they put it down to mark their ball on the green?

Most of the time it is superstition. Many pros have quirks in marking a ball on the green with a coin in a certain manner. Some always place the coin heads up with the face looking at the hole. Others are making sure that they are using their lucky coin. If they have to move their mark for another player, many will flip the coin to remind themselves to move it back to the original spot before they putt.

The Course

One of golf's unique features is that no two playing fields in the world are alike. Subtle changes brought about by wind, rain, sun or the growth of grass can have pronounced effects on the game. Golf's architects have continually blended nature and the spirit of the game to create character and challenge in the holes that they have built.

From St. Andrews to the stadium courses of today, the gold course has served as a test of strategy and skill that is seldom found in any other arena. The playing fields themselves—Muirfield, Troon, Baltusrol, the Country Club—have earned sacred spots in golf lore and legend. The courses are sources of controversy and debate, love and respect, fear and dread. Golfers relive courses as soldiers relive battlefields. Certain holes live in fame and infamy for the deeds performed on them. Though the course is the opponent, it must be the most loved opponent in the annals of sport.

The Course

Why is it said that "putts always break toward the water"?

It is not that the water has some magnetic force on the ball. Water, of course, seeks its lowest level, which is usually a body of water—an ocean, lake or pond near the green. As water drains toward the body of water it tends to shape the slope toward the direction of the pond or lake. Additionally, the grain on the green tends to grow in the direction of a water source. These factors cause a putt to break in the direction of a body of water.

The Course

Why is "The Country Club" of Brookline so named?

The site of the 1988 U.S. Open has been referred to as The Country Club since its beginning. It was built as a "park where members may be free from the annoyances of horse railroads and meet for pleasure, driving and riding." The club was formally established in 1882. The Country Club gained fame when a young Francis Ouimet won the 1913 U.S. Open in a playoff against Harry Vardon and Ted Ray.

Why do many golf courses in Japan have two greens per hole?

The Japanese climate has extreme ranges in temperature. Bent grass, the preferred grass for greens, tends to burn out quickly in the hot, humid summers. To solve this problem, the Japanese decided to build two greens per hole. One green would have bent grass, which would be regrown each year. The other green would be of korai, a very tough grass imported from Korea which can withstand harsh winters. Thus, Japanese clubs offer their members two greens, one for summer and one for winter.

The Course

Why is the famous Olympic Course in San Francisco called "the course that was built in reverse"?

In 1922 the Olympic Club, a private social club, purchased a course near Lake Merced called Lakeside. The course was located on the bare side of a large hill that ran down to the lake. The Olympic Club immediately began planting eucalyptus, pine and cypress trees to outline each of the eighteen holes. The trees matured some twenty-five years later to become an essential part of the challenge and beauty of Olympic. That trees were planted on an existing course rather than having holes carved out from a forest gave birth to the expression "built in reverse."

The Course

Why are there "dogleg" holes?

Dogleg holes were first designed about sixty years ago to break the monotony of straightaway holes and afford the golf architect some leeway in matching design characteristics and golfing skills. The dogleg hole may tempt the long hitter to cut over trees or water to gain a closer approach shot. Additionally, bunkers, rough, water and trees can be strategically placed on a dogleg to reward the great shot and punish the stray one as few straight holes could.

Why are there so many tee locations and so much teeing space at most courses?

The amount and location of teeing ground determine the leeway architect and greenskeeper have when planning shotmaking and maintenance. Nine-hole courses often have significant differences in the tee-markers from front to back nine to bring variety and afford players the challenge of hitting different shots on the same hole. In championship conditions, the tee locations may be used to add distance and increase the level of difficulty of a hole. To set a course record, a competitor must use the back tees.

The Course

Why are flagsticks all the same height?

The USGA recommends that the flagstick be a minimum of seven feet high. Manufacturers generally adhere to this size because of perspective. If flagsticks varied in height from course to course it would be difficult to judge distance.

The Course

Why is the stretch between the eleventh and thirteenth holes at Augusta National called "Amen Corner"?

The origin of the term "Amen Corner" is unknown, but many pros believe that if you can negotiate these three holes in par a prayer is in order. The three holes have had a long history in deciding the Masters. The eleventh is 445 yards, with water to the left and behind the green. The second shot is usually a 4- to 6-iron that must be strategically placed. The twelfth is a par 3 of only 155 yards, but wind conditions and pin placement make this one of the most difficult holes on the course. The thirteenth is a 485-yard dogleg par 5. Water runs the entire left side and crosses in front of the green. The water and traps surrounding the green give pause to the long hitters who try to hit this green in two.

Why are the tees that are farthest back called "tiger tees"?

Very good golfers were once commonly referred to as tigers, poor ones as rabbits. The very good players would naturally play from the back tees.

The Course

Why is one trap at Oakmont called "Church Pews"?

Between the third and fourth holes at Oakmont there is a trap that is 60 yards long that is set to catch stray drives from both holes. The trap has seven grassy ridges that run across it giving the appearance of church pews.

Why is the fourth hole at Baltusrol famous in golfing lore?

Baltusrol hired the famous golf architect Robert Trent Jones to toughen up the course for the 1954 U.S. Open. After he finished his task by making alterations on several holes, the members complained that he had made the course too tough. The new fourth hole, for example, required a tee shot of almost 200 yards across water to a well-bunkered par 3. Jones, along with the club pro, club president and the chairman of the Open committee, actually played the fourth hole to rate its toughness for themselves. After the first three had hit their shots, Jones teed up and holed out the shot for an ace. He simply shrugged: "As you can see, gentlemen, this hole is not too tough."

The Course

Why is Pine Valley often considered the top golf course in the United States?

Pine Valley, located in Clementon, New Jersey, places a premium on accuracy and distance that few courses can match. Many of the holes at Pine Valley do not have continuous fairways but rather narrow and demanding landing areas. Stray shots do not land in simple rough: sandy scrub brush and water abound along the landing areas. The par 3s demand that the ball land and hold the green, and the par 5s average around 600 yards and require three perfect golf shots to get home.

The Course

Why is the eighteenth tee at Harbour Town called "Nicklaus tee"?

Harbour Town Golf Links, located on Hilton Head Island in South Carolina, is the site of the Heritage Golf Classic. The eighteenth hole has several tees, but one is located in a position that requires a drive of 250 yards to a peninsula portion of the fairway. This tee is not used too often in tournament play because of its extreme difficulty. Many Harbour Town members say it would take one of Jack's drives just to reach the fairway.

Why do greenskeepers use the term "put to bed" in regard to a golf course?

Greenskeepers in the north "put the course to bed" in late fall. The procedure usually entails covering the greens to prevent damage from frost and ice, placing snow fences around greens and tees to prevent skiers or snowmobiles from cutting tracks into the turf, and digging special drainage ditches for traps or particularly wet spots along the course. The purpose, of course, is to survive the winter in good shape and be ready for an early opening in the spring.

The Course

Why is the sand trap on the seventh hole at Pine Valley called "Hell's Half-acre"?

The seventh hole at Pine Valley has been called the most exacting par 5 in the world. Its 585-yard length is not the real problem: the huge expanse of sand and scrub brush that begins 285 yards off the tee and extends for over 100 yards creates one of the most challenging holes in the game. In order to play this hole in par, you have to hit a grassy landing area on the second shot that is 385 yards from the tee. In other words, it takes two very long and accurate golf shots just to be in position to hit the green with the third. The giant sand trap that defines this golf hole is in the Guinness Book of World Records as the world's largest sand trap and is affectionately known as "Hell's Half-acre."

Why is the famous golf course Baltusrol so named?

Located in Springfield, New Jersey, Baltusrol's name is derived from a farmer of Dutch origin named Baltus Roll, who once owned the land.

The Course

Why are some courses characterized as "championship"?

A championship course is one that presents situations that a championship caliber player must be able to execute. It should require both distance and accuracy and it should force strategic moves on the part of the competitor. It should also place a degree of difficulty on the finesse shots and reward consistent putting.

Why are those new, very short courses called "Cayman" courses?

Cayman courses, which run around 4,000 yards in length, were first put into use in the Cayman Islands. Special balls that travel a shorter distance than normal are used to play these courses. Cayman courses rose out of the shortage of land tracts required for a full-length course and the steady growth in the number of golfers each year. The first Cayman courses were developed in the early 1980s.

The Course

Why does the ball seem to sit up better on the fairways of Florida courses?

Most of the courses in Florida use Bermuda grass, a wiry, coarse-bladed grass that grows well in warm climates. Because Bermuda grass is so thick, it holds the ball up on the fairway much more effectively than grasses such as Poa annua or bent.

Why is the sixteenth hole at Firestone called "The Monster"?

The sixteenth at Firestone is a 625-yard par 5. While downhill, the advantage of the slope is negated by the lie usually left for the long second shot home. Water guards the green in front, prohibiting even the boldest player from firing at the green from a distant, downhill lie. Legend has it that only two players have ever hit the green in two in competition—Firestone's club pro and former PGA Champion Bobby Nichols and Arnold Palmer. It was Arnold Palmer who used the word "monster" to describe the hole after he took a triple-bogey 8 on it in the 1960 PGA Championship.

When holes are rated for strokes, why are some difficult holes rated lower than holes that seem easier?

Difficulty is not necessarily the main criterion in deciding which holes are to be considered the stroke holes in an order from one to eighteen. The USGA's guidelines call for consideration to be given to a poorer player in a match against a superior player, so that the main criterion is the place where the player needs the stroke the most. Also, the stroke holes are distributed equally on the front and back nines (odd-numbered on the front, even-numbered stroke holes on the back). Though the holes on one nine may be tougher than on the other, the stroke holes still must be distributed equally. Generally holes are graded in the following order: difficult par 5s, difficult par 4s, remaining par 5s, remaining par 4s and par 3s. Of course, exceptions may be made for especially tough par 3s and 4s.

The Course

Why is Oakmont famous for its sand traps?

Oakmont opened in 1904 with an incredible 350 bunkers, almost twenty per hole. In order to cut maintenance costs the number was gradually cut to 171.

Why are some courses called "stadium" courses?

Stadium courses are specifically designed to accommodate large galleries for PGA Tour events. Many of the older courses on the tour are surrounded by trees or water that prohibit galleries from getting a good view of the golf action. Stadium courses are designed with large slopes around the greens, viewing perches, walking paths and other facilities to facilitate large groups of golf fans and offer them a better view of play.

The Course

Why do some courses have wicker baskets instead of flags on their flagsticks?

Originally flagsticks were just plain staffs. Eventually they sported small disks with the number of the hole on them. Most flagsticks at the turn of the century were about three feet tall. The Sunningdale Course in England used wicker baskets to help golfers see the pin placement better from any angle. The wicker-basket pins were also very popular in England because they did not aid the golfer in determining the strength and direction of the wind. Hugh Wilson designed Merion Golf Club near Philadelphia in 1912. Wilson studied course architecture in England and was impressed with the British tradition. He thought the addition of wicker baskets at Merion would help establish it as a unique course in the United States. Some courses have copied Merion's flagsticks, but the wicker-basket pins are relatively scarce because of cost and maintenance.

The Course

Why are some courses called "executive" courses?

Because executive courses are shorter than championship courses, they can be played more quickly, and the busy executive can get a round into his schedule. But the main reason for the rise in the executive course is the scarcity of good golf-course land and the great increase in people playing golf.

Why is Wack-Wack, a course on the Asian Tour, so named?

Often the site of the Philippines Open, Wack-Wack Golf and Country Club is located near Manila. It got its name from the sound of crows, which were extremely numerous and bothersome to the players in the early days of the course.

The Rules

On May 14, 1754, the Honourable Company of the Royal and Ancient Club was formed and developed thirteen articles that have served as the basis for the rules of play that we use today. The Rules of Golf command the allegiance of the world's golfers. Few sports can boast the intrinsic sense of honesty required by the game itself. In what other sport do competitors call penalties upon themselves without reservation? The Rules of Golf are always, however, being tested by new situations, rubs of the green and technological advances in equipment. The Rules serve to keep the game as a sport defined by skill and based on fairness to all who tee it up.

The Rules

Why are there fourteen clubs?

Theoretically, if there were no limit to the number of clubs a player could have a club for every possible contingency and thus have an unfair advantage over the competition. The USGA and the Royal and Ancient agreed on fourteen because it represented a standard set of clubs—2- through 9-irons, a wedge, a putter and four woods.

Why can a player repair ball marks but not spike marks on a green?

This rule was designed to prevent a player from gaining a distinct advantage by tamping down a groove on his ball's line to the hole. Because spike marks are so common, a player could repair a series of them and create a depression that could affect the roll of the putt. Repairing spike marks would slow the game down considerably. The marks created by the impact of a ball, on the other hand, can create a significant and unfair obstacle for a putt.

The Rules

Why do players drop a ball at an arm's length rather than over their shoulder as they used to do?

The modification in the Rules had several intents. While dropping a ball for relief, a player would often bounce it off of his shoulder or heel by accident, so that the ball landed outside the drop area. The drop over the shoulder also often caused players to toss the ball rather than drop it. By extending one's arm for the drop, the likelihood of the ball remaining in the intended drop area is increased.

Why is there a rule against grounding a club in a sand trap?

Rule 13-4 prohibits the touching of soil, sand or any living thing in a hazard as a means of preventing testing the texture and thereby gaining an unfair advantage. A hazard is considered a form of punishment for a stray shot. Testing the sand or soil would partially negate the effect of the "punishment."

Why is there a rule against "building a stance"?

If there were not a rule against building a stance a player could take measures that would certainly be unfair. For example, a golfer faced with a downhill lie could use a small pedestal or fill in the ground to make his stance level. Players could also use devices to help them push off their back foot. The rule is intended to make everyone play the course as intended.

The Rules

Why does Rule 10 state that players who play out of turn in stroke play will be disqualified if their intent was to give an advantage to a player? What is the advantage?

The rule is intended to prevent two or three players agreeing to hit first in order to help someone. The scenario might go as follows: Two players are hopelessly out of the hunt in a stroke tournament. Their good friend Bob is only a few shots back with five holes to go. As a favor for their friend, they agree to hit before Bob. Bob is able to see what clubs were hit, how the ball travels in a wind condition, and how it reacts upon landing. This type of behavior would be a serious breach of the Rules and a common sense of fairness and deservedly carries the penalty of disqualification for those involved.

The Rules

Why do the Rules of Golf place so much emphasis on amateur and professional status?

The Rules of Golf have almost ten pages on the status of amateur and professional. The main emphasis is on fairness. It would not be fair for someone who derives his living from the game to play against those who play golf as an avocation. Much of the attention the Rules give to status is the definition of what constitutes being a professional and how one may apply for reinstatement as an amateur.

Why is there a difference between a water hazard and a lateral water hazard in the Rules?

If a ball lands in a water hazard the Rules call for the player to drop a ball behind the water hazard and to keep the spot at which the ball crossed the water hazard between the player and the hole. In many cases, such as a wide river or ocean inlet, it is not practical or possible to do this. Lateral water hazards are marked with red stakes, and a ball should be dropped within two club lengths of the point where it entered the hazard.

The Rules

Why can't a player go to an adjoining sand trap, take a swing to test the consistency of the sand, then step into the trap in which his ball lies and play it?

This practice would not be in keeping with the spirit of the game and is prohibited by the Rules. Rule 13-4a states that "a player shall not . . . test the condition of a hazard or similar hazard."

Why is there a rule against using foreign materials on a golf ball?

Rule 5-2 was written with the intention of preventing a player from gaining an unfair advantage by using a substance that could change the flight characteristics of the ball. For example, a ball sprayed with a slippery substance does not have as much sidespin, so that hooks and slices can be avoided. Such actions, not dependent on golfing skill, are outlawed.

Why do some scorecards have a figure called "slope" on them?

Handicaps may vary from course to course, depending on length and difficulty. Every player should have a USGA handicap expressed in strokes and a fraction of a stroke as well as the handicap that he carries at his home course. If a player travels to a new course he or she may convert the USGA handicap into a course handicap by using the Course Handicap Table on the scorecard or posted in the clubhouse which is known as the "slope."

Why are pin placements made as they are in tournaments?

There are no specific rules in regard to the location of pins. Greenskeepers, however, use some general guidelines of fairness and common sense in cutting the holes. At most PGA tournaments the holes are usually cut six on the left, six on the right and six in the middle so as not to favor players who prefer to draw or fade their shots into the green. Greenskeepers also keep the ground flat around the cup and consider the type of shot required to get the ball close.

The Rules

Why is the term "through the green" used in the Rules?

The term "through the green" is used repeatedly' in the Rules to denote the entire area of the course with the exception of the teeing area and putting green of the hole being played. There is no reference to the terms "fairway" and "rough" in the Rules of Golf. The word "green" was synonymous with a golf course in the early days of golf.

Why are tournament officials concerned with time in golf?

The Rules of Golf mention time several times. Although advocates of the game love the lack of a clock, in tournament golf time comes into play: a ball is lost if it is not found within five minutes; failure to start on time may result in disqualification (though if the player arrives within five minutes he may be penalized two strokes in stroke play or lose the first hole in match play); and finally there are penalties (two strokes in stroke play, loss of hole in match play) for undue delay on the course.

Why can't a caddie hold an umbrella over his player while he putts?

Rule 14-2 (assistance) states: "In making a stroke, a player shall not accept physical assistance or protection from the elements." The rule is intended to prevent one player who has special equipment or help over someone who does not. This rule, as most rules, is designed to restrict competition to golfing skill and not the result of gimmicks or special advantage.

The Rules

Why can't you move a hazard stake that interferes with your swing when you cannot remove an out-of-bounds stake in a similar situation?

A hazard stake is an obstruction. Whether it is movable or not depends on how it is installed. Objects defining out-of-bounds are not obstructions and cannot be removed.

Why is it difficult for a touring pro to revert back to amateur status?

All professionals who seek to become amateurs must apply to the USGA for reinstatement and then undergo a two-year waiting period. However, the Rules of Golf state that "players of national prominence who have acted contrary to the Definition of an Amateur Golfer for more than five years normally will not be eligible for reinstatement."

The Rules

Why are the rules-making meetings called "quad-rennial conferences"?

The Rules of Golf are formulated in a joint effort between the Royal and Ancient Golf Club of St. Andrews and the United States Golf Association. Delegates from the two associations meet twice a year to review proposed changes. The rule book, however, is published only every four years, thus the name "quadrennial" is affixed to the conferences.

The Rules

Why is a stroke counted for a player who swings
and misses the ball because the wind blew it off
the tee before the clubhead arrived?

Rule 11-2 states that a ball may be reteed if it falls
off the tee while addressing it. However, once a
player makes a stroke—"a forward movement of
the club made with the intention of fairly striking
at and moving the ball"—it is indeed counted.

Why don't the touring pros use binoculars to
survey the area for their shots?

Rule 14-3 prohibits artificial devices and unusual
equipment. Such items as range-finders and survey
equipment would greatly take away from the spirit
of the game and give too much prominence to
technology over golfing skill.

The Rules

Why do the Rules allow practice on the course before a match play event but not stroke play?

According to Tom Meeks, director of Rules and Competitions for the USGA, there are no specific reasons why you can practice in the one case but not in the other. In fact, the note at the end of Rule 7-1 permits the Committee to reverse this rule. Mr. Meeks goes on to explain that the main reason why practice is permitted in match play is that there are only two players. In stroke play the numbers would be so large that practicing on the course could be a big administrative problem, and the maintenance crew might not be able to complete its work.

The Rules

Why is so much emphasis placed on club design in the Rules of Golf?

Five very specific pages in the Rules of Golf detail the permissible design of clubs in order to keep the game one of skill rather than one of technology. The flight characteristics of a golf ball can be greatly influenced by such design modifications as the width between grooves on an iron, the mass of the clubhead, flex characteristics of a shaft and the material of an insert into the clubface. The basic idea is to preserve the game of golf as a function of a player's skill and not the result of advanced technology.

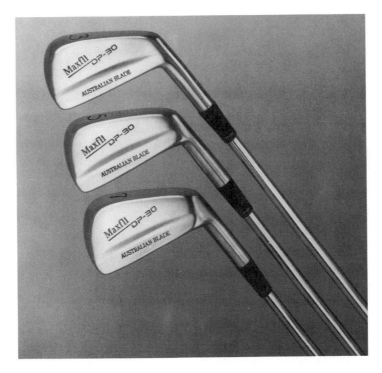

The Rules

Why do many pros hold their clubs out of the grass in the rough as they address the ball?

It is legal to ground your club anywhere on the course except in a hazard. However, if the ball moves after you have taken your address, there is a one-shot penalty. To address the ball under the Rules you must 1) take your stance and 2) ground the club. Many top players hold the clubhead a few inches from the ball so that technically they have not addressed the ball. Should the ball move in this situation, there is no penalty.

Why was croquet-style putting outlawed?

Rule 16-1e prohibits standing astride or on the line of a putt. Croquet-style putting enjoyed a brief period of popularity when Sam Snead used it to cure his "yips." The croquet style, however, was never a traditional golf stroke, and never considered a fair stroke. Additionally, a player would gain a distinct advantage by being able to sight directly down the line of a putt as compared to the traditional manner of putting. Rule 16-1e was put into effect to preserve the traditional and inherent fairness of the game.